The Greatest of These is Love

*A Resource for
Small Group Faith Sharing*

By Christopher J. Ruff, M.A., S.T.L.

- Discipleship Series -

Novo Millennio Press

The Greatest of These is Love

Novo Millennio Press
PO Box 160
La Crescent, MN 55947
www.novomill.com

Nihil obstat: Rev. Samuel A. Martin, S.T.L.
Censor Librorum

Imprimatur: Jerome E. Listecki, D.D., J.C.D.
Bishop of La Crosse
Nov. 1, 2008

The *nihil obstat* and *imprimatur* are official declarations that a book or pamphlet is free of doctrinal or moral error. No implication is contained therein that those who have granted the *nihil obstat* and *imprimatur* agree with the contents, opinions, or statements expressed.

Cover art:
El Greco, *St. Paul,* 1610-14.
Museo del Greco, Toledo, Spain.
Image licensed by B.P.A. Fine Art, FL.

Graphics and Design:
Alice J. Andersen
www.alicejandersen.com.

Foreword

In the summer of 2006, Christopher Ruff, director of the Office of Ministries and Social Concerns for our diocese, came to me with a proposal. He wanted to develop a diocesan small group faith-sharing program that would take the typical "Bible study" ingredients of prayer, reflective study and fellowship, and add one more—loving service.

Chris felt too many Catholics saw ministry to the suffering and needy as belonging only to Church social justice committees and institutions like Catholic Charities, with their own role reduced to giving these groups financial support. Of course it is true that Jesus tells the story of a Samaritan who gave money to an innkeeper for the care of a beaten man—but not before compassion had moved the Samaritan personally to clean the man's wounds with oil and wine and to lift him onto his own animal to bring him to that inn.

With this kind of love of neighbor in mind, Chris looked for a faith-sharing resource that would combine a prayerful, contemplative spirit with the universal call to serve Christ in "the least of his brethren." He wanted to find something that penetrated to the heart of the Gospel but that was concise, readable and workable for people with busy lives. Even the vital service component had to be manageable and broad enough to include various kinds of service. In the end, Chris decided to write his own resource, on his own time so he could publish it. He then wrote a second book, with a third in the works and more planned.

The response in the Diocese of La Crosse has been extraordinary.

In what was supposed to be a small pilot phase in Lent of 2007, over one thousand people in more than thirty parishes took part (in our modest Wisconsin diocese of 165 parishes). Concluding surveys reflected great enthusiasm and more than 95% said they wished to continue with the next resource. As the program was made available to the entire diocese with the second book in the fall of 2007, nearly two thousand people joined groups in close to one hundred parishes.

This expanding set of faith-sharing resources is aptly named the Discipleship Series. I am seeing it form disciples in our diocese—integral and authentic disciples growing in love of God and love of neighbor. It is my hope that in the planting and nurturing brought about through this Discipleship Series, we will look forward to a harvest of apostolic works. I recommend it wholeheartedly to individuals, groups, parishes and other dioceses that wish to foster a deeper discipleship in Christ.

Most Rev. Jerome E. Listecki
Archbishop of Milwaukee
(Written in 2008 as Bishop of La Crosse)

Acknowledgments

I would like gratefully to acknowledge the tremendous encouragement and support I have received from Bishop Jerome Listecki in the undertaking of this project.

I would also like to thank Alice Andersen for her skilled editing and design.

Finally, and most of all, I would like to thank my wife Clare, whose love for Christ shines out, and who continues to show great patience with my late nights at the keyboard.

Christopher Ruff

Table of Contents

Introduction *(page 9)*

How to Use This Book *(page 12)*

Biographical Sketch of St. Paul *(page 17)*

Year of St. Paul – Prayer of Pope Benedict XVI
  (page 20)

Opening Prayer to the Holy Spirit *(page 21)*

Session 1 - Amazing Grace *(page 22)*

> *The Lord in His Scriptures – The Conversion of Saul*
> *Pope Benedict XVI Quote and Catechism n. 448*
> *The Lord in the Life of His People – An Unlikely Apostle*
> *Questions for Discussion*
> *Closing Prayer – Ephesians 1:3-5;7-12*

Session 2 - We Are One Body *(page 42)*

> *The Lord in His Scriptures – Many Members, One Spirit,*
> * One Lord*
> *Pope Benedict XVI Quote and Catechism n. 2045*
> *The Lord in the Life of His People – A Broken Man Becomes*
> * a Beacon of Light*
> *Questions for Discussion*
> *Closing Prayer – Cardinal John Henry Newman*

Session 3 - The Greatest of These is Love
(page 60)

> *The Lord in His Scriptures – Paul's Tribute to the Highest*
> * Gift*
> *Pope Benedict XVI Quote and Catechism n. 1823*
> *The Lord in the Life of His People – Mother Teresa's Legacy*
> * of Love*
> *Questions for Discussion*
> *Closing Prayer – Inspired by St. Faustina Kowalska*

Session 4 - He Chooses the Lowly *(page 80)*

> *The Lord in His Scriptures – The Foolish Shame the Wise*
> *Pope Benedict XVI Quote and Catechism n. 544*
> *The Lord in the Life of His People – A Little Child Shall
>   Lead Them*
> *Questions for Discussion*
> *Closing Prayer – Prayer to St. Maria Goretti*

Session 5 - For the Sake of the Gospel *(page 98)*

> *The Lord in His Scriptures – Embracing the Heart of a
>   Servant*
> *Pope Benedict XVI Quote and Catechism nn. 24, 25*
> *The Lord in the Life of His People – I Make Myself a Leper
>   with the Lepers to Gain All to Jesus Christ*
> *Questions for Discussion*
> *Closing Prayer – Prayer to St. Damien of Molokai*

Session 6 - Transformed by His Cross *(page 116)*

> *The Lord in His Scriptures – Nothing Can Separate Us from
>   the Love of Christ*
> *Pope Benedict XVI Quote and Catechism n. 2844*
> *The Lord in the Life of His People – Forgiveness Lights a
>   Path of Hope*
> *Questions for Discussion*
> *Closing Prayer – For Those Who Suffer for the Name of
>   Christ*

Appendix – Suggestions for Service *(page 134)*

Introduction

Welcome to *The Greatest of These is Love,* part of the Discipleship Series of faith-sharing resources.

The aim of this book, and of the series in general, is to foster shared prayer and reflection that bears fruit in loving action; in that it differs from a linear, more academic "Bible study."

The focus here is to:

- Soak deeply and prayerfully in a select number of Scripture passages.
- See the meaning of those passages come alive in human stories that inspire.
- Reflect as a group on discussion questions that apply to daily living.
- Foster a modest commitment to love of neighbor through service.
- Experience the fullness of joy that only Christ can give!

In just over twenty years of organizing and writing materials for faith-sharing groups, these are the fruits I have come to see and expect. The component of active love of neighbor comes from the conviction that true discipleship must take seriously Jesus' words, "Whatever you did for the least of my brethren, you did for me" (Mt 25:40). And truly the fruit of love is joy.

As support for this approach, I turn to Jesus' allegory of the Vine and the branches (John 15:1-17). We have all heard it many times, with its image of Jesus the Vine, to whom we as branches must be joined if we are to bear fruit. I encourage you to read it again and to consider some key phrases:

"Abide in me . . . abide in my love."

Let ". . . my words abide in you."

". . . that you bear much fruit, and so prove to be my disciples."

"Love one another as I have loved you."

". . . that my joy may be in you, and that your joy may be full." (see verses 4-12)

I believe we can find in these forty-six words of Jesus the very essence of his Gospel, his call to us. And the faith-sharing approach of the Discipleship Series is an attempt to respond actively and enthusiastically to that call. *"Abiding" bears fruit in love, whose nectar is joy.*

But what of St. Paul, the subject of this book? Actually, the true subject of this and all books in the Discipleship Series is Jesus Christ, but in fact St. Paul and his words are paths to the Lord. And if we have been painting a picture of oneness with Christ, we have already been painting a picture of Paul, who wrote in his letter to the Galatians, "It is no longer I who live, but Christ who lives in me" (2:20).

From the moment of his encounter with the Lord on the Road to Damascus, Paul was seized by Christ and full of passion for his Gospel. He poured out his life spreading that Gospel, enduring countless sufferings along the way, culminating in martyrdom.

Paul's words to the men and women of the churches he founded burned with the fire of loving concern, correction, exhortation. Those words speak to us as they first spoke to them. Indeed, as Pope Benedict XVI urged in his homily inaugurating the "Year of St. Paul" (June 28, 2008): "Let us not ask ourselves only: who *was* Paul? Let us ask ourselves above all: who *is* Paul? What does he say to me?"

Let us listen and abide. And may the fruit of our abiding be a fuller, more charitable, more joyful discipleship that moves the world to marvel, as the ancient pagans did: "See how they love one another!"

Christopher Ruff

How to Use This Book

The Discipleship Series of faith-sharing materials aims to be simple and flexible. What follows is everything you need to know to move forward:

Establishing and Running One or More Groups

- Through personal invitation or parish announcements, form one or more small groups (5-12 people each).

- If established for Lent, the groups should meet weekly. Otherwise, once a month tends to be more workable for most people's schedules. Typical length for a session is about 90 minutes. Whatever time frame is established, it should be rigorously respected.

- Each group should have a facilitator. It can be the same person at each meeting, or the facilitator role can rotate.

- The job of the facilitator is not to be an expert in the material or to do a lot of talking. Rather, it is to start and end the meeting on time, to help keep things moving and on topic, and to foster a friendly, supportive environment in which everyone feels invited to contribute.

- The group members decide where they would like to meet. It is ideal to hold the sessions in each other's homes since a key goal is to bring faith into daily life. If this is not workable, a room on church grounds is fine, or some combination of the two.

- Each member is expected to read the material prayerfully ahead of the session, jotting a few notes in response to the "Questions for Discussion."

- The session begins with the Prayer to the Holy Spirit or some other appropriate prayer so that hearts may be opened to God's presence.

- The group members then read aloud the material for that session, taking turns reading small sections. This pattern should continue all the way through the discussion questions.

- When there are about ten minutes left in the allotted schedule, it is time to proceed to the "Group Prayers of Intercession," even if the group has not finished all the discussion questions.

- The prayers of intercession are intended to be spontaneous prayer intentions. They direct the power of prayer to various needs and simultaneously deepen the spirit of fellowship in the group. Conclude with the "Closing Prayer."

- The session should end on time, even if members are eager to keep going. This is vital for the health and longevity of the group. It is good to follow with fifteen or twenty minutes of social time for those who are able to stay. Simple refreshments are a nice touch, with emphasis on the word simple; otherwise, people feel pressure to keep up with high expectations.

The Service Component

- The Service Component distinguishes this program from many other faith-sharing approaches. It is anticipated that group members will devote an hour or two to some form of service between sessions (if meetings are weekly, this could be an hour or two each month). The service may be carried out individually or together with others.

- Service can take many forms, but it should come from the heart. Certainly service to the poor, the sick, the elderly, the homebound, the homeless, etc., has always had a privileged place for Christ's followers.

- Some may already be devoting a great deal of time to service. In that case, it is enough to consciously "dedicate" some portion of that service to the group's communal effort and spirit.

- Each set of "Questions for Discussion" includes at least one that touches on the component of service. This is to keep alive the awareness of the importance of the service aspect, which however is done on the "honor system" (with no one watching over anyone else's shoulder).

Group Etiquette

- Pray for the members of your group between sessions.

- Maintain confidentiality.

- Be a good listener and encourage everyone to contribute to the discussion, without anyone monopolizing. Members that are more talkative should allow everyone a chance to respond before they speak a second time.

- Love your neighbor by speaking charitably and refraining from any kind of gossip.

- Be on time, come prepared, and actively take part in discussion and prayer.

- Take seriously the service component so that you may be a loving (and always humble) witness to the others in your group.

- Be open and expect God's action in your life and prayer—expect to be changed!

A Biographical Sketch of St. Paul

St. Paul was born in approximately 8 AD (hence the anniversary "Year of St. Paul" declared by Pope Benedict XVI for 2008) in Tarsus, the capital of the Roman province Cilicia, in what is now Turkey. He was both a Jew and a Roman citizen and had two names—Saul, his Jewish/Hebrew name, and Paul, his Roman/Latin name. In the Acts of the Apostles, Luke refers to him as Saul until 13:9, where he shifts to Paul. No explanation is given, but it may be intended to signal Paul's mission as Apostle to the Gentiles.

At age 12 or 13, Paul left Tarsus for Jerusalem to be taught by the renowned Rabbi Gamaliel, a strict Pharisee. In his letter to the Galatians, Paul recalled: "I advanced in Judaism beyond many of my own age among my people, so extremely zealous was I for the traditions of my fathers" (1:14). It is not surprising, then, that he viewed the movement started by Jesus of Nazareth as a threat to Jewish orthodoxy. Three times in his letters he admits he proudly "persecuted the Church of God" (1 Cor 15:9; Gal 1:13; Phil 3:6). In fact, when we first meet Paul in Acts 7:58, he is guarding the robes of those stoning St. Stephen to death.

Everything changed for Paul upon his dramatic

encounter with Christ on the road to Damascus (Acts 9:1-19), which took place in approximately 36 AD. Powerfully transformed, this man who had zealously persecuted Christians would become an even more zealous preacher of Christ and the Gospel in what we know today as Israel, Syria, Turkey, Greece, Italy and possibly Spain. His travels are typically clustered into three main missionary journeys.

Wherever Paul went, he preached first in the synagogues and then to the Gentiles. Viewed as a dangerous traitor by the Jewish authorities, Paul was often persecuted and threatened with death. Yet he was able to found numerous churches, and his thirteen letters, which make up nearly a third of the New Testament, consist mostly of his correspondence with these Christian communities. These letters, written roughly between 50 and 67 AD, are generally held to be the earliest New Testament writings we possess. It is possible that a few did not have Paul as their actual author (the letters to Timothy and Titus are the most disputed), but the Pauline tradition behind them is strong.

Paul was arrested and imprisoned or kept under house arrest several times, and Ephesians, Philippians, Colossians, and Philemon are known as his "captivity letters." He was ultimately martyred in Rome, probably under Nero in about 67 AD.

It is worth noting in conclusion that Paul dictated his letters. That spontaneity helps us understand the passion of his words as he pours out the feelings and concerns of his heart. Pledged to celibacy, he had no children of his own, yet he felt himself a father to the people of the churches he founded, and his paternal love and zeal light up his words. Inspired by the Holy Spirit, those words are just as capable of touching us today. As Pope Benedict XVI declared: "For us Paul is not a figure of the past whom we remember with veneration. He is also our teacher, an Apostle and herald of Jesus Christ" (Year of St. Paul, Inaugural Homily, June 28, 2008).

Pope Benedict XVI

Let us . . . thank the Lord for having called Paul, making him the light to the Gentiles and the teacher of us all, and let us pray to him:

> Give us even today witnesses of the Resurrection, struck by the impact of your love and able to bring the light of the Gospel in our time. St Paul, pray for us! Amen.

(Year of St. Paul, Inaugural Homily, June 28, 2008.)

Recommended prayer to start each session:

Prayer to the Holy Spirit

Come Holy Spirit,
Fill our hearts with the fire of your love.

Draw us near to Jesus,
so that we may witness to his presence
in every moment of our lives.

Renew us, so that our homes, parishes,
neighborhoods and world
may be transformed into the heavenly
Father's kingdom on earth,
where love and mercy reign.

Amen.

Session 1

Amazing Grace

The Lord in His Scriptures

The Conversion of Saul

. . . Saul, still breathing threats and murder against the disciples of the Lord, went to the high priest and asked him for letters to the synagogues at Damascus, so that if he found any belonging to the Way, men or women, he might bring them bound to Jerusalem. Now as he journeyed he approached Damascus, and suddenly a light from heaven flashed about him. And he fell to the ground and heard a voice saying to him, "Saul, Saul, why do you persecute me?" And he said, "Who are you, Lord?" And he said, "I am Jesus, whom you are persecuting; but rise and enter the city, and you will be told what you are to do." The men who were traveling with him stood speechless, hearing the voice but seeing no one. Saul arose from the ground; and when his eyes were opened, he could see nothing; so they led him by the hand and brought him into Damascus. And for three days he was without sight, and neither ate nor drank.

Now there was a disciple at Damascus named Anani'as. The Lord said to him in a vision, "Anani'as." And he said, "Here I am, Lord." And the Lord said to him, "Rise and go to the street called Straight, and inquire in the house of Judas for a man of Tarsus named Saul; for behold, he is praying, and he has seen a man named Anani'as come in and lay his hands on him so that he might regain his sight." But Anani'as answered, "Lord, I have heard from many about this man, how much evil he has done to thy saints at Jerusalem; and here he has authority from the chief priests to bind all who call upon thy name." But the Lord said to him, "Go, for he is a chosen instrument of mine to carry my name before the Gentiles and kings and the sons of Israel; for I will show him how much he must suffer for the sake of my name."

So Anani'as departed and entered the house. And laying his hands on him he said, "Brother Saul, the Lord Jesus who appeared to you on the road by which you came, has sent me that you may regain your sight and be filled with the Holy Spirit." And immediately something like scales fell from his eyes and he regained his sight. Then he rose and was baptized, and took food and was strengthened. For several days he was with the disciples at Damascus.

And in the synagogues immediately he proclaimed Jesus, saying, "He is the Son of God." And all who heard him were amazed, and said, "Is not this the man who made havoc in Jerusalem of those who called on this name? And he has come here for this purpose, to bring them bound before the chief priests." But Saul increased all the more in strength, and confounded the Jews who lived in Damascus by proving that Jesus was the Christ. **Acts 9:1-23.**

Soak in the Word.

Two Minutes of Silence.

Reflect . . .

This is where it all begins for Paul . . . a 180 degree turn, a completely new life.

One minute he is Saul the Pharisee, zealous and sure of himself, armed with a mission, determined to stamp out the dangerous sect established by Jesus of Nazareth—in Saul's eyes, an executed Jewish heretic.

The next minute—a blinding flash of light, the sensation of falling, and that unforgettable voice: "Saul, Saul, why do you persecute me?"

"Who are you, Lord?"

"I am Jesus . . . ."

In that moment it is all over. Blind and helpless, Saul needs to be led by the hand into the city. He humbly bows to the orders he receives from Jesus. How remarkable to think this is the man who in Acts 8 was seen gladly approving of the murder of Stephen and dragging Christian men and women from their homes to be thrown into prison.

Saul denies himself food and drink for three days, then receives the Holy Spirit and Baptism. At last his eyes are opened, he sees.

The old Saul has died, a new man is born. Is it any wonder the theme of dying to sin and rising to new life would become so dear to him? He has met his Lord. He would refer to Jesus with that title, "Lord," a total of 275 times in his letters, far more than any other New Testament writer.

Each time he invoked it, one wonders, did he remember that day on the road when he first begged to know—"Who are you, Lord?" Did the answer still take his breath away . . . ?

" . . . I am Jesus."

What about me? Have I heard his voice in my heart? Have I met Him—really met Him—along the road of my life?

Pope Benedict XVI

Paul's faith is being struck by the love of Jesus Christ, a love that overwhelms him to his depths and transforms him. His faith is not a theory, an opinion about God and the world. His faith is the impact of God's love in his heart.

(Year of St. Paul, Inaugural Homily, June 28, 2008.)

Turning now to ourselves, let us ask what this means for us. It means that for us too Christianity is not a new philosophy or a new morality. We are only Christians if we encounter Christ. Of course he does not show himself to us in this overwhelming, luminous way, as he did to Paul . . . . But we too can encounter Christ in reading Sacred Scripture, in prayer, in the liturgical life of the Church. We can touch Christ's Heart and feel him touching ours. Only in this personal relationship with Christ, only in this encounter with the Risen One do we truly become Christians.

(Year of St. Paul, General Audience, September 3, 2008.)

Catechism of the Catholic Church

448 - Very often in the Gospels people address Jesus as "Lord." . . . At the prompting of the Holy Spirit, "Lord" expresses the recognition of the divine mystery of Jesus. In the encounter with the risen Jesus, this title becomes adoration: "My Lord and my God!" It thus takes on a connotation of love and affection that remains proper to the Christian tradition: "It is the Lord!"

The Lord in the Life of His People

An Unlikely Apostle

From bitter enemy to fervent apostle. That is the story of St. Paul. It is also the story of Bartolo Longo. Though his remarkable journey would take place more than 1800 years later and differ from Paul's in significant ways, both witness to the amazing power of God's grace.

It was the 1860's and Bartolo Longo was studying law at the University of Naples, where St. Thomas Aquinas had studied and taught six centuries before. But times had changed, and now it was full of revolutionary ideas and anti-religious faculty. Under these influences, it wasn't long before Bartolo brushed aside his Catholic upbringing, calling it "childhood nonsense" and declaring that he "grew to hate monks, priests and the pope." With his hardened heart, he welcomed every opportunity to speak harshly of the Church of his youth. And yet there was an emptiness in his soul that hungered for a deeper meaning to life.

Into darkness . . . and back

It was then that a friend introduced Bartolo to the occult. He began attending séances and conversing with spirits that spoke through a psychic medium in a trance. He was so intrigued he decided he wanted to become a priest of the occult. After a period of initiation, he was "consecrated" in a bizarre midnight ritual. From that point he began to experience the presence and guidance of a being he called his "angel."

But the messages and instructions Bartolo and his like-minded friends received from their spirit guides contradicted each other (besides contradicting the Gospel), and he entered a dark period of confusion, sadness and nervous exhaustion. It would be wrong to characterize him as a satanist, for Bartolo believed he was dealing with "elevated" spirits. But the diabolical source was evident in its fruits—he had lost his faith and was on the verge of losing his sanity.

Bartolo was rescued from his downward spiral by one of the few remaining devout Catholic professors at the University—Professor Vincenzo Pepe. Professor Pepe warned Bartolo of the dangers of his occult path. He prayed for him and introduced him to a holy Dominican priest, Fr. Alberto Radente, who met daily with Bartolo. Gradually the scales fell from the young man's eyes and he made a good confession and his first Communion in many years.

Charity and the Rosary

Bartolo soon met another holy priest, Fr. Louis da Casoria, a man completely dedicated to helping the needy and the oppressed. This "Mother Teresa" of

Naples radiated gentleness, humility and joy. Fr. Casoria's witness of love captivated Bartolo and radically affected the course of his life. He would later write: "This extraordinary man who founded churches and hospices has been our teacher in charity . . . a living testimony of faith."

Bartolo began to visit dying patients in the hospital. It was now clear to him that while his fascination with the occult had brought him nothing but dark self-absorption and anxiety, the charity of the Gospel fostered humility, generosity and peace. About the same time, Bartolo began to pray the Rosary with friends. These would be the hallmarks of the rest of his life—charity and the Rosary.

At the age of thirty-one, Bartolo made an eye-opening trip to Pompeii on business as an attorney. Never had he encountered such wretched poverty, along with religious ignorance and superstition. When he visited the parish church, he found it infested with pests and falling apart. He had to do something.

A shrine and a legacy of compassion

In 1876, Bartolo began a humble effort to build a new church. This would culminate eleven years later in the magnificent Shrine of Our Lady of the Rosary of Pompeii. Donations poured in, many miracles were recorded, and devotion to the Rosary spread like fire, well beyond the confines of Pompeii.

Bartolo would later marvel: "We wanted to provide for the religious life of poor peasants; we succeeded instead in producing a truly universal movement of faith."

But every bit as spectacular as the Shrine was the charitable work done by Bartolo Longo. After the example of Fr. da Casoria, he could no longer look at the world without seeing the afflicted and asking himself how he could help. And so he founded a school for impoverished young children, noting that the first need was to "wash their faces and rid them of the insects attacking their fragile bodies." He also established an orphanage for girls, founding an order of women religious to care for them.

It broke Bartolo's heart to see the plight of many boys who were not orphans but whose fathers were in prison. The experts of the day declared these boys doomed to a life of crime, but Bartolo didn't agree and founded a home for them. Years later hundreds of these boys had passed through the home and grown into virtuous, successful men. The secret? Bartolo wrote: "I gave them, and taught them to love, Jesus Christ."

Bartolo Longo died peacefully on the morning of October 5, 1926. He was 85. Fifty-four years later he was beatified by Pope John Paul II, who called him "the apostle of the Rosary, the man of Our Lady."

Through the mercy of God, Bartolo Longo, like St. Paul, had undergone a most radical conversion, from bitter enemy of Christ's Bride the Church, to intimate friend, "chosen instrument," ardent apostle.

Pope John Paul II on Blessed Bartolo Longo

Bartolo Longo is the apostle of the Rosary, the layman who fully lived his Christian commitment. . . . He can truly be defined as "the man of Our Lady": for love of Mary he became a writer, an apostle of the Gospel, propagator of the Rosary, founder of the famous Shrine . . . for love of Mary he created institutes of charity, he became a beggar on behalf of the children of the poor, he transformed Pompeii into a living citadel of human and Christian goodness."

(Homily at Mass of Beatification, October 26, 1980.)

Questions for Discussion

1. As Saul makes his way to Damascus he swaggers with powerful resolve ("breathing threats and murder against the disciples of the Lord"). But at the moment of his stunning encounter with Jesus he is rendered blind and helpless and must then be "led by the hand" into Damascus by his traveling companions. How does this humbling experience prepare him for the new mission he will receive from the Lord? Are there lessons we can draw from it?

2. Jesus bursts into Saul's life in a spectacular way on the road to Damascus, but then he sends Anani'as to restore his sight and bring him into the Christian community. Why do you think our all-powerful God makes use of mere human instruments like Anani'as—or you and me—when he could do it all himself?

_____

_____

_____

_____

_____

_____

3. When Anani'as expresses fear about following
   God's command to go and meet Saul, God reas-
   sures him by telling him that Saul is his "chosen
   instrument" for spreading the Gospel. In what
   ways did God use Bartolo Longo as a chosen instrument in his plan? In what sense is each of us a
   chosen instrument?

   _____

   _____

   _____

   _____

   _____

   _____

   _____

   _____

4. Discuss the similarities and the differences between the conversion stories of Saul of Tarsus and Bartolo Longo.

_____

_____

_____

_____

_____

_____

_____

5. The charitable example and influence of Fr. Louis
   da Casoria was particularly powerful in the life of
   Bartolo Longo.

   • How did it affect him and what fruit did it bear?
   • Has anyone impacted you in this way?
   • Discuss ways we can give that kind of example
     to others.

_____

_____

_____

_____

_____

_____

_____

_____

_____

6. Bartolo Longo became a fervent apostle of the Rosary. What do you think it is about the Rosary that has made it such a beloved devotion in the lives of so many of the faithful, from the simplest peasants to the greatest Popes?

_____

_____

_____

_____

_____

_____

Group Prayers of Intercession

8 to 10 minutes

Closing Prayer

Ephesians 1:3-5;7-12

Blessed be the God and Father of our Lord Jesus
  Christ,

Who has blessed us in Christ with every spiritual
  blessing in the heavens,

as he chose us in him, before the foundation of the
  world,

to be holy and without blemish before him.

In love he destined us for adoption to himself
  through Jesus Christ,

in accord with the favor of his will. . . .

In him we have redemption by his blood, the forgiveness of transgressions,

in accord with the riches of his grace that he lav-
  ished upon us.

In all wisdom and insight, he has made known to us
the mystery of his will
in accord with his favor that he set forth in him
as a plan for the fullness of times, to sum up all
things in Christ,
in heaven and on earth.

In him we were also chosen,
destined in accord with the purpose of the one
who accomplishes all things according to the inten-
tion of his will,
so that we might exist for the praise of his glory,
we who first hoped in Christ.

Amen.

Session 2

We Are One Body

The Lord in His Scriptures

Many Members, One Spirit, One Lord

. . . [J]ust as the body is one and has many members, and all the members of the body, though many, are one body, so it is with Christ. For by one Spirit we were all baptized into one body—Jews or Greeks, slaves or free—and all were made to drink of one Spirit. For the body does not consist of one member but of many.

If the foot should say, "Because I am not a hand, I do not belong to the body," that would not make it any less a part of the body. And if the ear should say, "Because I am not an eye, I do not belong to the body," that would not make it any less a part of the body. If the whole body were an eye, where would be the hearing? If the whole body were an ear, where would be the sense of smell? But as it is, God arranged the organs in the body, each one of them, as he chose. If all were a single organ, where would the body be?

As it is, there are many parts, yet one body. The eye cannot say to the hand, "I have no need of you," nor again the head to the feet, "I have no need of you." On the contrary, the parts of the body which seem to be weaker are indispensable, and those parts of the body which we think less honorable we invest with the greater honor, and our unpresentable parts are treated with greater modesty, which our more presentable parts do not require. But God has so composed the body, giving the greater honor to the inferior part, that there may be no discord in the body, but that the members may have the same care for one another. If one member suffers, all suffer together; if one member is honored, all rejoice together. Now you are the body of Christ and individually members of it. **1 Corinthians 12:12-27.**

Soak in the Word.

Two Minutes of Silence.

Reflect . . .

Rivalry is as old as fallen human nature. Jesus had the exasperation of dealing with it even among his chosen disciples. Indeed, in Luke 9:44-48 we see that just after he told them he would be betrayed, the disciples started to argue about who was the greatest!

In 1 Corinthians, we see Paul addressing rivalries in the Christian community he had founded about 50 A.D. in Corinth, one of the most cosmopolitan towns in the Roman world. Being a port city open to both East and West, Corinth was always buzzing with different ideas and philosophies, and these at times had an impact on Christian beliefs and practices.

Then there were differences in ethnicity and class. The Church in Corinth was made up mostly of Gentiles but included a number of Jewish Christians; and it came mainly, but not only, from the poorer classes. On top of that, while Paul was the chief evangelizer of the community, he was not the only one. In particular, a Christian preacher by the name of Apollos had captivated many people with his charismatic style.

Given weak human nature, these differences erupted into factions and rivalries. The underlying themes are sadly familiar to every age: Whose group is the most important, the most gifted, the closest to true doctrine?

Hence Paul's reflection on the Body of Christ made up of many members. The spirit pervading that Body must not be jealousy and competition, but love. Echoing Jesus (see Luke 9:49), Paul says that in some sense the least members are the greatest. And if the Body is characterized by love, the members share each other's joys and sufferings.

How often in our personal lives and even in our parishes do we see factions, rivalries, jealousy? We may be tempted at times to throw up our hands in frustration. But instead, when we discover these weaknesses, especially in ourselves, we ought to reflect quietly on Scriptures like 1 Corinthians and ask God to touch us with his grace, purify our hearts, and grant us humility.

May our greatness be found in our littleness and in the charity of our hearts and our actions. May we love the entire Body of Christ in all its members, but with special attention to the neglected, the lowly and the poor. That message was needed 2000 years ago, and it is needed today.

Pope Benedict XVI

To the Corinthians, among whom discord had arisen, St. Paul does not hesitate to address a strong call for them all to remain in agreement, for there to be no divisions among them, and for them to unite in the same mind and purpose (cf.1 Corinthians 1:10). In our world, the phenomenon of globalization is being consolidated, yet, despite this, persistent divisions and conflicts continue, men and women feel a growing need for certainty and peace. . . . Only in Christ and in his Gospel can humanity find the answer to its deepest hopes."

(Year of St. Paul, Audience with Orthodox Patriarch Bartholomew I of Constantinople, Saturday, June 28, 2008.)

Catechism of the Catholic Church

2045 - Because they are members of the Body whose Head is Christ, Christians contribute to building up the Church by the constancy of their convictions and their moral lives. The Church increases, grows, and develops through the holiness of her faithful, until "we all attain to the unity of the faith and of the knowledge of the Son of God, to mature manhood, to the measure of the stature of the fullness of Christ."[3]

---

[3] *Eph.* 4:13; cf. *LG 39.*

The Lord in the Life of His People

A Broken Man Becomes a Beacon of Light

In the Body of Christ there are holy members renowned for wondrous lives and deeds, for mysticism and miracles. We praise God for them. Then there are those who could pass almost unnoticed. They remind us weak and ordinary folk that our calling is no less sublime. Such a one was Matt Talbot.

The workday done, young Matt Talbot sat at O'Meara's Tavern with his friends, drunk as usual, when the money ran out. It had happened before, and since alcohol was his life, Matt would do whatever it took to get more. Once he had even pawned his boots and had to walk home in his stockings.

This particular evening a blind fiddler was making music at O'Meara's. When he set his fiddle down, Matt snatched it up and ran to the pawn shop, returning with more money for drink. His friends thought it a fine joke and so did Matt. It was only after the party broke up that the blind man found the source of his livelihood was missing.

Flash forward. . . . Matt Talbot's eyes scan the streets of Dublin. It is years since he has had a drink and his days are now filled with prayer and peace.

But there is a memory he can't erase. "Lord help me, help me find that blind man." Perhaps today, on the street corner—is that him?

He never finds him. The painful memory, like a thorn in his side, remains. He has Masses said for the man in restitution.

A hard beginning

Matt Talbot was born in Dublin, Ireland, to an alcoholic father in 1856. He was one of twelve children. The family was poor. At the age of twelve, Matt went to work at a firm that bottled beer, where he began drinking the dregs at the bottom of returned bottles. In two years he graduated to whiskey and by the time he was sixteen he came home drunk regularly. Beatings from his father failed to stop him. The word in the neighborhood was, "Poor Matt! Oh, he's going to the Devil!"

In his twenties, Matt spent all his wages and spare time at O'Meara's Tavern. His friends had many vices, but his was only one—the bottle.

Then at twenty-eight, a humiliation changed Matt's life. He had been out of work for a week and was broke. Since he had always been generous with his drinking friends, he felt sure he could expect the same. So he stood outside O'Meara's Tavern as they entered. They passed him one by one and left him standing on the corner.

The turning point

Matt slowly made his way home, "cut to the heart," as he would say years later. His mother was preparing the mid-day meal when he arrived, and was stunned to see him sober.

"Ma, I'm going to take the pledge for life," he said. In nineteenth century Ireland it was common for someone who wished to stop drinking to take a solemn pledge before a priest to abstain for a period of time. Matt found a priest and made his first confession in three years. The priest persuaded him to take the pledge for ninety days only.

Those three months were an agony of withdrawal. To fill the time he used to spend at O'Meara's, Matt went for walks and often stopped in churches. He began attending Mass and receiving Communion daily, which in that era was very unusual. He slept little, fasted, and read the lives of the saints and other spiritual writings. At the end of three months, he took the pledge to abstain from alcohol for six months and finally for life.

Matt didn't talk much about his struggles with alcohol, but once shared with a friend about a day, early on, when he had wandered crazy and desperate through the streets of Dublin, in and out of churches, unable to pray. Finally he had flung himself on the steps of a church with his arms

outstretched, not caring what anybody thought.
At last peace came and he entered and was able to
pray.

Remembering a humble man

Matt was a conscientious employee and one of his
foremen called him "the best worker in Dublin." A
fellow worker said he was "strong as a little horse"
and "smiled at everything except a dirty joke." He
considered marriage once, but concluded in prayer
that it wasn't the Lord's path for him.

Many coworkers experienced Matt's generosity.
He lent them money to buy clothes or shoes for their
children or to pay overdue rent. He gave generously
to the missions, too, spending next to nothing on
himself.

This humble, anonymous little man died suddenly
of a heart attack at the age of 69, as he was making his way to Sunday Mass. No one recognized the
frail body lying in the middle of Granby Lane. Four
days later he was identified by his sisters, who had
reported him missing. Little by little, his hidden but
remarkable story came to light, and in 1975, Pope
Paul VI declared him "Venerable," the first step on
the path to canonization.

From the world's point of view, Matt Talbot was
unremarkable, a nobody, even a little odd. But as
one humble member of the Body of Christ, he shone

brightly and gave glory to God. All over the world today, addicts and their families turn to him for intercession and hope—hope that they too, with the grace of God, can emerge victorious.

Pope Paul VI

You have chosen to look upon Matt Talbot as an admirable exemplar of discipline and supernatural virtue. It is our hope that his success will encourage countless men and women throughout the world to realize the need for conversion, the possibility of real rehabilitation, the serenity of Christian reconciliation, and the peace and joy of helping others to overcome abuses, disorders and sin.

(Address to Members of Calix Society, May 11, 1974.)

Questions for Discussion

1. What do we share as Catholic Christians that makes us One Body in Christ? Think of as many realities or facets as you can.

_____

_____

_____

_____

_____

_____

_____

2. In 1 Corinthians 12:12-27, it is clear that one
   thing Paul is trying to do is convert his hearers
   from jealousy and pride. Why do we have such
   a tendency to want to look at ourselves and our
   group as "better" than others? What are some
   remedies for that?

   _____

   _____

   _____

   _____

   _____

   _____

   _____

   _____

3. As you carry out the component of loving service in this faith-sharing program, have you considered that some "unfortunate" persons in need of care and compassion may be Matt Talbots, just needing the right influence to become radically good and holy? How might this impact your approach to service?

_____

_____

_____

_____

_____

_____

4. Discuss the lessons all of us can take from the life of Matt Talbot.

_____

_____

_____

_____

_____

_____

_____

5. Addiction tends to lead to isolation, to a turning in on oneself and one's cravings for the addicting substance or "high." The addict becomes less and less able to connect meaningfully with others. What do you think a Christian man or woman can do to try to reach someone in this condition (recognizing that ultimately we can't control another person's free will)?

_____

_____

_____

_____

_____

_____

Group Prayers of Intercession

8 to 10 minutes

Closing Prayer

God has created me to do Him some definite service;

He has committed some work to me which He has
  not committed to another.

I have my mission—I may never know it in this life,
but I shall be told it in the next.

I am a link in a chain, a bond of connection between
  persons.

He has not created me for naught.

I shall do good, I shall do His work;

I shall be a preacher of truth in my own place,
while not intending it, if I do but keep His command-
   ments
and serve Him in my calling.

Therefore, my God, I will put myself without reserve
   into your hands.

What have I in heaven, and apart from you what do
   I want upon earth?

My flesh and my heart fail, but God is the God of my
   heart, and my portion forever.

Prayer of Cardinal John Henry Newman (1801-1890.)

Session 3

The Greatest of These is Love

The Lord in His Scriptures

Paul's Tribute to the Highest Gift

If I speak in the tongues of men and of angels, but have not love, I am a noisy gong or a clanging cymbal. And if I have prophetic powers, and understand all mysteries and all knowledge, and if I have all faith, so as to remove mountains, but have not love, I am nothing. If I give away all I have, and if I deliver my body to be burned, but have not love, I gain nothing.

Love is patient and kind; love is not jealous or boastful; it is not arrogant or rude. Love does not insist on its own way; it is not irritable or resentful; it does not rejoice at wrong, but rejoices in the right.

Love bears all things, believes all things, hopes all things, endures all things. Love never ends; as for prophecies, they will pass away; as for tongues, they will cease; as for knowledge, it will pass away. For our knowledge is imperfect and our prophecy is imperfect; but when the perfect comes, the imperfect will pass away.

When I was a child, I spoke like a child, I thought like a child, I reasoned like a child; when I became a man, I gave up childish ways. For now we see in a mirror dimly, but then face to face. Now I know in part; then I shall understand fully, even as I have been fully understood. So faith, hope, love abide, these three; but the greatest of these is love. **1 Corinthians 13:1-13.**

Soak in the Word.

Two Minutes of Silence.

Reflect . . .

Poetic as it is—and oh so popular at weddings—
Paul wrote this hymn to charity as a kind of correction to the Christians of Corinth. They had become
overly fascinated with spectacular gifts of the Holy
Spirit, like speaking in tongues, prophecies and mys-
tical phenomena. This aura of mystery and spectacle
was part of Greek culture with its pagan rituals,
oracles and secret knowledge, and it was tempting
for recent converts from that culture to gravitate to
those elements.

Not that extraordinary gifts were bad. When
genuine, they were a sign of the Spirit that was to
accompany the Messiah (see Joel 3:1) and that was
poured out at Pentecost. Paul understood that God
could and did bestow them, but not for their excitement value or prestige. Paul wanted the Corinthians
to see that the proof of true Christian mysticism is
not sensational phenomena but the interior grace of
the Holy Spirit. And the only sure sign of this grace
is a life of charity, a life of love.

Furthermore, all the gifts—whether the unspec-
tacular ones of governing or teaching, or the more

obviously supernatural gifts like healing, prophecy or tongues—are meant by God to serve the good of the whole Christian community, not the individual through whom they manifest. A wonder-worker who says "Look at me!" is not being led by the Spirit of God.

So Paul is saying to the Corinthians, and to us today: Do not be seduced or puffed up by sensational spiritual phenomena, or by any gift or talent God has given you. Do not give in to the desire to be noticed or praised. Pray for one gift above all others—the gift of love! And in a world that has become confused about the meaning of love, reducing it to a feeling, to the flutter of romance, use the "litmus test" provided by 1 Corinthians 13:1-13. If it makes it through that checklist, it is love indeed, a precious gift from God.

Pope Benedict XVI

Paul is presented by many as a pugnacious man who was well able to wield the sword of his words. Indeed, there was no lack of disputes on his journey as an Apostle. He did not seek a superficial harmony. . . . But what most deeply motivated him was being loved by Jesus Christ and the desire to communicate this love to others. Paul was a man capable of loving and all of his actions and suffering can only be explained on the basis of this core sentiment.

(Year of St. Paul, Inaugural Homily, June 28, 2008.)

Catechism of the Catholic Church

1823 - Jesus makes charity the new commandment.[4] By loving his own "to the end,"[5] he makes manifest the Father's love which he receives. By loving one another, the disciples imitate the love of

---

[4] *Cf. Jn* 13:34.
[5] *Jn* 13:1.

Jesus which they themselves receive. Whence Jesus says:

> "As the Father has loved me, so have I loved you; abide in my love." And again: "This is my commandment, that you love one another as I have loved you."[6]

St. Teresa of Avila (1515-1582)

Christ has no body now on earth but yours,

No hands but yours, no feet but yours,

Yours are the eyes through which

He looks with compassion on this world;

Yours the feet with which he walks to do good;

Yours the hands with which he blesses.

---

[6] *Jn* 15:9,12.

The Lord in the Life of His People

Mother Teresa's Legacy of Love

If you asked people today to give you the name of one person synonymous with self-giving love, most would probably say Mother Teresa of Calcutta. As the following story illustrates, the love exemplified by Blessed Mother Teresa lives on in the Missionaries of Charity she founded.

Sister Francesca, one of the earliest members of the Missionaries of Charity, answers quickly when asked what made her join Mother Teresa and the fledgling congregation 57 years ago.

"Mother's eyes," she said instantly. Mother Teresa gave her a searing look, and "I could not escape," she continued. "It was stronger than the sun. It burned everything inside me. The world was gone, the world was burnt out." All that remained was "God's world, the world of love."

"I spent my life, burnt out my life," she said.

And is she happy?

"Very happy," she said. "I made a good choice."

Sister Francesca was the ninth young woman to join Mother Teresa in 1950, four months before the official founding of the Missionaries of Charity. Today she belongs to the community at St. Rita's Convent in the South Bronx. Another sister there, Sister Dorothy, who entered in 1949, was the fourth to join Mother Teresa.

Sisters Francesca and Dorothy, together with their provincial, Sister Leticia, and their local superior, Sister Regis, spoke about their life and their founder.

They say they still feel close to her.

"In our work and in our religious life, we feel Mother's presence," Sister Dorothy said.

A different kind of poverty

It was in 1971 that Mother Teresa established a mission in Harlem—her first in North America. A year later they would establish their own convent in the Bronx, and then relocate to St. Rita's in 1973.

"Mother felt the need to serve the poorest of the poor in this rich country," said Sister Dorothy, "because she thought poverty in this country was quite different from poverty in India." The worst poverty in the United States, she explained, is "loneliness, unwantedness, not being loved."

In Harlem, the Missionaries of Charity began visiting shut-ins and others in their homes, helping them with housecleaning and cooking.

"No one ever visited them," Sister Dorothy said. "Some of them called the sisters 'angels.' They said, 'Angels are coming to visit us.' "

Gifts of love

At St. Rita's, the sisters visit families in their homes and run food pantries. Donations come from "divine providence," the sisters said. The credit goes to God.

"He asks us to care for his people. We concentrate on that, and he provides, totally," Sister Leticia said. Speaking about donors, she remarked, "Mother Teresa loved the American people. They are so loving, so generous, so concerned for the poor."

The sisters also operate a temporary shelter for men, a soup kitchen, and a summer day camp. Shelter guests stay for two weeks, and only overnight; after breakfast they must leave. Some meet with social workers. Sister Leticia said that some get into trouble again, but that does not discourage the sisters, because there always is the chance that someone might turn his life around.

Said Sister Leticia, "One soul is worth everything, no?"

Mother Teresa established an AIDS residence in Manhattan in 1985. Sister Dorothy said the first patient was a prisoner, and Mother Teresa was warned by prison officials that if they released him to her care, she was responsible to see he did not escape. She offered to take his place if he did. Sister Dorothy laughed at the memory.

The idea of Mother Teresa in a prison lineup would make just about anyone laugh, but she must have meant the offer—and she must have made it with a twinkle in her eye.

The man was a lapsed Catholic who experienced "a great conversion" while being cared for by the sisters, Sister Dorothy added. "Within a couple of months he died in peace," she said.

"Mother was a woman of God," said Sister Dorothy. "She had great, great love for Jesus. Everything she did was for Jesus. She taught us that when we are working among the poorest of the poor, we are touching the body of Jesus . . . we see the face of Jesus."

To quench His thirst

In the sisters' chapel is one of the congregation's symbols, a large crucifix with the words "I thirst"—spoken by Christ from the cross—painted on the wall beside it.

"In the present-day Calvary, we discover the thirst of Jesus in the poorest of the poor," Sister Dorothy continued. "We make them aware that

Jesus is thirsting for them, and help them to respond to his thirst, to his love. That is our work, that is our apostolate. . . . This is the whole aim of our society."

Sister Leticia explained that Mother Teresa made it clear the Missionaries of Charity are not social workers.

"The most important thing is that we bring Jesus to the poor, take Jesus where he has never walked before," she said. Smiling, she added that when the sisters visit families, children sometimes call them "Mrs. God," or say, "God is here."

"It is so beautiful to see that, and to hear that," she said, "to be able to bring God to the poor and to love him in this way, through the poor."

(Condensed from: "Ten years after Mother Teresa's death, her spirit lives on in her sisters." By Claudia McDonnell for Catholic New York, 9/6/2007. Reprinted with permission.)

Pope Benedict XVI

Anyone who needs me, and whom I can help, is my neighbor. . . . Jesus identifies himself with those in need, with the hungry, the thirsty, the stranger, the naked, the sick and those in prison. . . . Love of God and love of neighbor have become one: in the least of the brethren we find Jesus himself, and in Jesus we find God.

(Encyclical *God is Love,* n. 15.)

Questions for Discussion

1. Paul wrote 1 Corinthians 13:1-13 because many of the Christians of Corinth were preoccupied with sensational gifts like speaking in tongues or uttering prophecy, and they were overlooking the absolute centrality of love. One could say that these tendencies have not changed much in two thousand years. How do you explain this?

_____

_____

_____

_____

_____

_____

2. In Paul's beautiful hymn to love, he describes this greatest of virtues both in terms of what it is and what it is not. Come up with ten or twelve of the attributes he identifies. Which strike you as most beautiful or moving? Which strike you as most difficult or challenging? In each case, why?

3. This faith-sharing program includes a component
   of service. Take a few moments to share ideas and
   discuss some of the ways members of your group
   have been trying to serve.

_____

_____

_____

_____

_____

_____

4. Obviously service can be carried out more or less
mechanically or out of a rigid sense of duty, or it
can be performed with love. What helps you to
carry it out with love?

_____

_____

_____

_____

_____

_____

5. What are one or two of the greatest examples of
   love you have ever seen or heard about? Discuss
   what you found especially striking about them.
   Feel free also to mention one or two memorable
   moments of love (especially sacrificial love) you
   have witnessed in your own family or community.

_____

_____

_____

_____

_____

_____

_____

6. A reporter who followed Mother Teresa of Calcutta around for a day said to her, "Mother, I wouldn't do what you do for a million dollars." Mother Teresa responded, "Neither would I." Discuss.

_____

_____

_____

_____

_____

_____

Group Prayers of Intercession

8 to 10 minutes

Closing Prayer

Lord Jesus, help me to be a living reflection of your love.

May my eyes be loving, that I might never judge harshly from appearances, but look for what is beautiful in my neighbor.

May my ears be loving, that I might be attentive to the needs of others and never be indifferent to their pleas or cries of pain.

May my tongue be loving, that I might speak words of kindness, encouragement, mercy and forgiveness.

May my hands be loving, that I might reach out to work, to serve, to comfort and to heal.

May my feet be loving, that I might hurry to the side of the abandoned or distressed.

May my heart be loving, that I might feel the joys, the hopes and the sorrows of my neighbor as my own.

Lord Jesus, help me to be a living reflection of your love.

Amen.

Inspired by a prayer of St. Faustina Kowalska (1905-1938).

Session 4

He Chooses the Lowly

The Lord in His Scriptures

The Foolish Shame the Wise

Do you not know that you are God's temple and that God's Spirit dwells in you? . . . God's temple is holy, and that temple you are.

Let no one deceive himself. If any one among you thinks that he is wise in this age, let him become a fool that he may become wise. For the wisdom of this world is folly with God. . . . For it is written, "He catches the wise in their craftiness . . . ."
1 Corinthians 3:17-19.

. . . God chose what is foolish in the world to shame the wise, God chose what is weak in the

world to shame the strong, God chose what is low and despised in the world, even things that are not, to bring to nothing things that are, so that no human being might boast in the presence of God. He is the source of your life in Christ Jesus, whom God made our wisdom, our righteousness and sanctification and redemption; therefore, as it is written, "Let him who boasts, boast of the Lord."
1 Corinthians 1:27-31.

Soak in the Word.

Two Minutes of Silence.

Reflect . . .

Corinthian culture was Greek culture, and the Greeks were proud of a deep heritage of philosophy and "wisdom." For people today, Plato and Aristotle are the most recognizable names in what is a star-studded list of ancient Greek philosophers.

It ran deep in Greek culture to love sophisticated debate and the mix of fascinating and subtle ideas. Paul recognizes this and had even tried, in Athens, to engage his Greek listeners on their own terms (see Acts 17:22-34).

But Paul discovers that while his Greek listeners are fascinated up to a point, they regard his preaching of Christ crucified as "foolishness," just as the Jews had so often found the cross to be a "stumbling block" (1 Corinthians 1:23).

And so Paul puts aside subtle reasoning and tells them that their sophistication, their "wisdom," is really foolishness and pride, and that true wisdom dwells only in the humble.

It brings to mind the words of Jesus: "I thank thee, Father, Lord of heaven and earth, that thou hast hidden these things from the wise and understanding and revealed them to babes" (Matthew 11:25).

Pope Benedict XVI

. . . [O]ne discovers that God is certainly "exalted" and transcendent, but he looks on the "lowly" with affection while he turns his face away from the proud as a sign of rejection and judgment (Psalm 138:6) . . . . [W]e too must know what choice to make, what the option is: to side with the humble and the lowliest, with the poor and the weak.

(General Audience, December 7, 2005.)

Catechism of the Catholic Church

544 - The kingdom belongs to the poor and lowly, which means those who have accepted it with humble hearts. Jesus is sent to "preach good news to the poor"; he declares them blessed, for "theirs is the kingdom of heaven." To them—the "little ones"—the Father is pleased to reveal what remains hidden from the wise and the learned. Jesus shares the life of the poor, from the cradle to the cross; he experiences hunger, thirst and privation. Jesus identifies himself with the poor of every kind and makes active love toward them the condition for entering his kingdom.

The Lord in the Life of His People

A Little Child Shall Lead Them

The story of Maria Goretti gives eloquent testimony to St. Paul's words about the weak, the foolish and the lowly shaming the "strong" and the "wise." It is no wonder that she is one of the Church's most beloved saints.

"No! No, Alessandro! It is a sin. God forbids it. You will go to hell, Alessandro!"

These are the cries of little Maria Goretti as twenty-year-old Alessandro Serenelli threatens her with a dagger, demanding that she give in to his desires.

It is an encounter between light and darkness, between purity and filth. Maria resists, fights him off. In his fury, Alessandro stabs her repeatedly and leaves her for dead.

She is eleven years old.

As "Marietta"—"little Maria"—lies dying in the hospital the next day, having made her last confession and Communion, the pastor of the local parish asks her if she is able to forgive her killer. She responds, "Yes, for the love of Jesus I forgive him, and one day I want him to join me in heaven."

Transformed by grace

Flash forward 32 years. . . . On his knees before Assunta Goretti is Alessandro Serenelli, murderer of her daughter. The day of the killing, the police had intervened to stop the townspeople from lynching him. Had he been one year older, he would have received the death penalty. But here he is at last, released from prison. "Please forgive me, Assunta," he pleads.

"Maria has forgiven you, God has forgiven you—I forgive you, too," says Assunta. She accompanies him to Midnight Mass and to Communion. It is Christmas.

Alessandro Serenelli lives the last 27 years of his life as a lay brother and gardener with the Capuchin friars of St. Seraphim. He testifies to Maria Goretti's holiness during her cause for beatification and is present with Assunta and a crowd of half a million at her canonization in 1950. When he dies peacefully at the age of 82, his last words are, "I am going to be with Maria."

"Don't worry, Mama"

Who was this Maria Goretti, and how did she become such a powerful channel of grace for her killer, as well as for untold numbers in this world who have sought her intercession to preserve or return to purity of heart and life?

Maria was the little girl who, just after losing her father to malaria at the age of ten, told her grief-stricken mother, "Don't worry, Mama. I will take care of the housekeeping chores while you take Papa's place in the fields. You will see, God will look after us."

She was remembered by the local baker as the girl who didn't eat the treats he gave her. One day he gave her a cookie, only to see her slip it into her apron. "Aren't you going to eat it?" he asked. Shaking her head, she smiled and answered, "The little ones will enjoy it." She was saving it for her younger sisters.

Maria was the pretty little girl who often went into nearby Nettuno ("Neptune") to sell eggs and chickens and to buy supplies for her family. While there she would visit the shrine of Our Lady of Graces and pray the Rosary for the repose of her father's soul. The other children of the village noticed her piety and referred to her, partly in mockery, partly in admiration, as the "little old lady." As the youngest child in her first Communion class, Maria gave a surprising answer to the priest who asked what she requested from Jesus after receiving Him. "Oh Father," she said, "I just asked to receive Him again!"

Fools for Christ

Maria and her family were poor and uneducated.
They had each other, their work in the fields, and
their daily Rosary. In the eyes of the world they
were nothing. Maria's father worked himself to an
early death, trying to earn a meager living as a joint
sharecropper with two men who lived on the other
side of the humble residence—Giovanni Serenelli
and his son Alessandro, whose pile of vulgar tabloids
was discovered one day by Assunta as she was clean-
ing. She feared to speak of it.

One could argue the Goretti's were poor fools.

But what was it Paul wrote? ". . . God chose what
is foolish in the world to shame the wise, God chose
what is weak in the world to shame the strong"
(1 Corinthians 1:27).

When Alessandro Serenelli went to prison for
killing Maria he was unrepentant. It is reported that
when someone told him the girl he murdered was
a saint, he replied with a sneer, "Then let her come
back from the dead."

A dream of lilies

If true, that was a challenge Maria must have
heard. After eight years of hardened prison life,
Alessandro had a dream he would never forget, a
dream that changed him to the core. Maria appeared

to him radiant in a field of flowers and began handing him white lilies. As he accepted them, each one became a still white flame.

As it happened, within a few days of this dream, the local bishop requested a meeting with Alessandro. The young man responded immediately with a letter welcoming the visit and begging God's pardon for the great sin he had committed.

In the end, Alessandro Serenelli had wielded a dagger, but Maria Goretti wielded the sword of the Spirit, the grace of God.

Reflect . . .

Who are the "wise" and the "strong" of our world today? Who are the ones who dominate our culture, the ones who try to seduce us with their counterfeit norms for success, excitement, entertainment?

In giving the answer to that question, one could grow cynical, but hope overcomes cynicism, good defeats evil, love conquers hatred and sin. That is what Maria Goretti teaches us, carrying the message of Calvary, where someone else was mocked as a fool and put to death. On the cross, in what appeared to be the very pit of powerlessness and humiliation, Christ won the definitive victory over sin and saved us all. In saints like Maria Goretti, little and humble, who have passed by way of that cross, his risen glory shines white as a lily, bright as a flame.

Pope John Paul II

"God chose what is foolish in the world to shame the wise, God chose what is weak in the world to shame the strong, God chose what is low and despised in the world, even things that are not, to bring to nothing things that are . . . ." (1 Cor. 1:27-29).

Yes, God chose her. Yes, God has clothed her with honor. He chose and clothed with honor a simple little country girl who was born poor. He clothed her with honor by the power of His Spirit. The natural person does not accept what pertains to the spirit of God, he does not accept because 'he cannot understand it;' rather, 'to him it is foolishness' (1 Cor. 2:14).

(Homily Commemorating 100th Anniversary of Birth of St. Maria Goretti.)

Questions for Discussion

1. Why does God privilege the lowly, the weak, and the despised in this world? What are some examples from the Bible?

_____

_____

_____

_____

_____

_____

_____

_____

2. St. Paul writes of the "wisdom" of the world that is really foolishness, and the "foolishness" of God's children that is really wisdom. What do you think are some examples from each side in today's world (consider persons, ideas, value systems, etc.)?

_____

_____

_____

_____

_____

_____

_____

_____

_____

3. If we reflect on these words of St. Paul about the
   weak and the lowly, what happens in our minds
   and hearts when we seek to serve people who are
   forgotten or suffering? What could be different
   about our experience of, say, an elderly man or
   woman in a wheelchair, a homeless person, or a
   child with Down syndrome?

   _____

   _____

   _____

   _____

   _____

   _____

4. Many lessons (for individuals and for society) can
   be drawn and applied from the life of St. Maria
   Goretti, as well as that of Alessandro Serenelli.
   What are some that occur to you?

_____

_____

_____

_____

_____

_____

_____

_____

_____

_____

5. At the Mass canonizing Maria Goretti in 1950,
Pope Pius XII would say to the huge crowd, ".
. . [A]ll of you who are intently listening to our
words, know that above the unhealthy marshes
and filth of the world, stretches an immense
heaven of beauty. It is the heaven which fascinated little Maria; the heaven to which she longed to
ascend. . . ."

- Is this message getting through today, especially to our young people? What hurts,
  and what helps?

_____

_____

_____

_____

_____

_____

_____

Group Prayers of Intercession

8 to 10 minutes

Closing Prayer

O holy little one of God, St. Maria Goretti.

So sweet, so humble, so pure of heart and life.

You were ordinary in the eyes of the world,

But remarkable in the eyes of faith.

Pray for us,

That in this proud and selfish and pleasure-seeking
world,

We may embrace the humility and radiant beauty of
the Gospel.

Though we may not die a martyr's death,

Pray God to grant us a martyr's heart,

Ready to embrace self-sacrifice for love of God and
   neighbor.
We ask you to intercede in a special way for our
   young people,
That they may know the serene joy of purity.
We pray this in Jesus' name.

Amen.

Session 5

For the Sake of the Gospel

The Lord in His Scriptures

Embracing the Heart of a Servant

[T]hough I am free from all men, I have made myself a slave to all, that I might win the more. To the Jews I became as a Jew, in order to win Jews; to those under the law I became as one under the law—that I might win those under the law. To those outside the law I became as one outside the law—not being without law toward God but under the law of Christ—that I might win those outside the law. To the weak I became weak, that I might win the weak. I have become all things to all men, that I might by all means save some. I do it all for the sake of the gospel, that I may share in its blessings. **1 Corinthians 9:19-23.**

[C]omplete my joy by being of the same mind, having the same love, being in full accord and of one mind. Do nothing from selfishness or conceit, but in humility count others better than yourselves. Let each of you look not only to his own interests, but also to the interests of others. Have this mind among yourselves, which is yours in Christ Jesus, who, though he was in the form of God, did not count equality with God a thing to be grasped, but emptied himself, taking the form of a servant, being born in the likeness of men. And being found in human form he humbled himself and became obedient unto death, even death on a cross.

Philippians 2:2-8.

Soak in the Word.

Two Minutes of Silence.

Reflect . . .

The first passage, taken from 1 Corinthians, is classic, passionate Paul. In the verses leading up to it he has just asserted his right to receive material support from the communities to whom he has been preaching the Gospel (see Jesus' words to his disciples in Mt. 10:10). But Paul declares that he has renounced this right. In fact, elsewhere we learn he made his living as a tentmaker (see Acts 18:1-3; 20:33-35; Philippians 4:14-16).

Just as he has renounced his right to material and financial support, here we see Paul renouncing his freedom, willingly becoming "a slave to all" for the sake of the Gospel.

Once again we see that, for Paul, Jesus is the center of everything, the reason for everything. If only he can win people to Christ, Paul will humble himself and accommodate himself to every type and class of person—the Jew under the Law of Moses, the Gentile not under that law, and those who are still weak or fragile in their Christian faith.

Paul does not mean he will make a false accommodation that would compromise the Gospel. He means he will meet people on their ground, in a way they can understand and relate to. He will not tower over them as some sort of superior being. Quite the opposite, he will humbly make himself "a slave" to them.

This takes us quite naturally to the famous passage from the letter to the Philippians about the self-emptying of Jesus.

Recall that man's original sin was disobedience born of the proud desire to make himself equal to God. The serpent had told Eve that if she and Adam would disobey and eat from the forbidden tree, "You will be like gods" (see Genesis 3:5).

It is fitting, then, that man's salvation would come through the exact reversal of that movement of proud disobedience. It would come because Christ, who was "in the form of God, did not count equality with God a thing to be grasped, but emptied himself, taking the form of a servant," becoming "obedient unto death, even death on a cross" (Philippians 2:6-8).

In short—man sins by arrogantly grasping for what is above him; Christ redeems by humbly becoming what is below him.

This is the example we are called to follow, says Paul. We should not consider our own interests and wishes, but those of others. We should be humble, not proud, and count others better than ourselves. We are called to empty ourselves, to give ourselves away in love.

All very simple, really, not complicated—just hard to do with a weak and fallen nature!

May the grace of Christ help us.

Pope Benedict XVI

Being open to Christ with all his heart, [Paul] had become capable of an ample dialogue with everyone, he had become capable of making himself everything to everyone. Thus he could truly be the Apostle to the Gentiles.

(Year of St. Paul, General Audience of September 3, 2008.)

. . . Paul gave himself to the Gospel with his entire existence; we could say 24 hours a day! And he exercised his ministry with faithfulness and joy, "that I might by all means save some" (1 Corinthians 9:22).

(Year of St. Paul, General Audience of September 10, 2008.)

Catechism of the Catholic Church

24 - "Whoever teaches must become 'all things to all men' (1 Cor 9:22), to win everyone to Christ. . . . [They] must suit their words to the maturity and understanding of their hearers, as they hand on the teaching of the mysteries of faith and the rules of moral conduct."[1]

25 - "Whether something is proposed for belief, for hope or for action, the love of our Lord must always be made accessible, so that anyone can see that all the works of perfect Christian virtue spring from love and have no other objective than to arrive at love."[2]

---

[1]*Roman Catechism,* Preface II; cf. *1 Cor* 9:22; 1 Pt 2:2.
[2]*Roman Catechism,* Preface 10; cf. *1 Cor* 13:8.

The Lord in the Life of His People

I Make Myself a Leper with the Lepers to Gain All to Jesus Christ

Many holy men and women throughout history have tried to imitate St. Paul in adapting themselves to the conditions and needs of the people to whom they ministered. But it would be hard to find a more heroic example than St. Damien of Molokai.

"I present Fr. Damien to you as one who will be a father to you, and who loves you so much that he does not hesitate to become one of you; to live and die with you."

These were the words Bishop Louis Maigret spoke on May 10, 1873, to the people of the lepers' colony of Kalaupapa on Molokai in the Hawaiian Islands. Fr. Damien de Veuster did not fear the saying that circulated about this island: "Prepare for Molokai as for the grave." No, the 33-year-old Belgian missionary priest had asked to be sent here.

The lepers' colony on Molokai was desperate and lawless and mostly neglected by the governing authorities. It needed someone like Fr. Damien. He brought order, the sacraments, and a fatherly love for this suffering people.

A sturdy compassion

Fr. Damien was no otherworldly saint. His temperament made him rough and direct at times, but also allowed him to accomplish much. He badgered the authorities for medicine and supplies, and under his leadership basic laws were enforced, shacks became painted houses, schools and churches and an orphanage were built. He himself slept outside under a tree for several weeks after his arrival, for he wouldn't take shelter until he saw that his people had sufficient huts of their own.

Fr. Damien had begun by visiting the lepers one by one. Their breath was foul; their bodies, already decomposing, gave off a horrible odor. One of his first visits was to a young girl. He found that worms had eaten her whole side. He had to overcome his natural repugnance for these sights and smells, and God gave him the grace to do so. His compassion for the afflicted men and women extended to dressing their sores, making their coffins and digging their graves.

In all this, Fr. Damien was sustained by the sacraments, especially the Eucharist. He wrote: "Without the constant presence of our Divine Master upon the altar in my poor chapels, I never could have persevered casting my lot with the lepers of Molokai."

Ministry of hope and joy

Fr. Damien taught the people to farm, to raise animals, to play musical instruments, to sing. Little by little, their accomplishments restored the sense of dignity their illness threatened to destroy. Funerals turned into processions of music and joy, as they began to feel the hope of resurrection. There were torchbearers, a band, and a choir. Because of the ravages of leprosy, it sometimes took two people to play the organ, so that together there would be ten fingers for the keyboard.

In 1883, seven Franciscan Sisters of Syracuse, led by Mother Marianne Cope, came to Molokai to help care for the lepers. Mother Marianne took charge of a home Fr. Damien had established for men and boys. She changed life on Molokai by introducing cleanliness, pride and fun to the colony. Bright scarves and pretty dresses for the women were part of her approach. The sisters continue to serve on Molokai to this day.

The final sacrifice

One evening in December of 1884, Fr. Damien was going about his usual ritual of soaking his feet in near-boiling water, when he noticed that he could not feel the heat. It was becoming clear to him that he had contracted leprosy. He bravely referred to the disease as his "shortcut to heaven," and continued to work vigorously even as his skin began to deteriorate. In one of his last letters prior to his death in 1889, he wrote: "My face and my hands are already decomposing, but the good Lord is calling me to keep Easter with Himself."

With his leprosy, Fr. Damien could now identify completely with his people, fulfilling what he had written to his brother six months after first coming to Molokai: ". . . I make myself a leper with the lepers to gain all to Jesus Christ. That is why, in preaching, I say 'we lepers'; not, 'my brethren. . . .'"

Fr. Damien died on April 15, 1889. The lepers to whom he had united himself set a black marble cross on his grave with the inscription, "Damien de Veuster, Died a Martyr of Charity." He was declared "Blessed" by Pope John Paul II on June 4, 1995, and canonized by Pope Benedict XVI on Oct. 11, 2009.

Testimony from beyond the Church

The life of St. Damien has touched many people and been the subject of books and films. Mahatma Gandhi claimed he was an inspiration for his social campaigns in India. One of the most powerful testimonies to this great man was given by the famed Scottish writer Robert Louis Stevenson *(Treasure Island, Kidnapped, The Strange Case of Dr. Jekyll and Mr. Hyde)*, a Presbyterian. Stevenson visited Molokai shortly after St. Damien's death and was struck by the people's love for him. He also came to know and admire Sr. Marianne Cope (herself beatified in 2005) and the other sisters. Just before he left the island, he presented them with a poem that provides a fitting end to this account of a life so beautifully poured out for others.

To the Reverend Sister Marianne,

Matron of the Bishop Home, Kalaupapa:

To see the infinite pity of this place,

The mangled limb, the devastated face,

The innocent sufferers smiling at the rod,

A fool were tempted to deny his God.

He sees, and shrinks; but if he look again,

Lo, beauty springing from the breasts of pain!

He marks the sisters on the painful shores,

And even a fool is silent and adores.

Pope John Paul II on St. Damien of Molokai

The certainty that *the only things that count are love and the gift of self* was his inspiration and the source of his happiness. The apostle of the lepers is a shining example of how the love of God does not take us away from the world. Far from it: the love of Christ makes us love our brothers and sisters even to the point of giving up our lives for them.

(Homily at Mass of Beatification, June 4, 1995.)

Questions for Discussion

1. It is clear that this session's passages from St. Paul were lived out by St. Damien of Molokai. What are some ways you can embody them as you seek to carry out the service component of this faith-sharing program?

_____

_____

_____

_____

_____

_____

_____

2. St. Paul speaks of becoming "all things to all men" for the sake of the gospel. Have there been times you have felt a need to adapt your way of sharing about the life and truth of Christ and his Church with someone, yet without watering down its fullness? Discuss.

_____

_____

_____

_____

_____

_____

_____

3. In his second letter to the Corinthians, St. Paul writes that God "comforts us in all our affliction, so that we may be able to comfort those who are in any affliction. . . . For as we share abundantly in Christ's sufferings, so through Christ we share abundantly in comfort too" (2 Corinthians 1:3-5).

- What do you think is this "comfort" that Paul is talking about?
- What do you imagine were sources of comfort for St. Damien?
- How can we become channels of God's comfort for others?

_____

_____

_____

_____

_____

_____

_____

_____

4. Obviously, St. Damien and the sisters who assisted him brought a Catholic presence to the suffering lepers of Molokai, with a spiritual ministry, prayer and the sacraments. But what else did they foster that was of great value to the people? Discuss.

_____

_____

_____

_____

_____

_____

Group Prayers of Intercession

8 to 10 minutes

Closing Prayer

[St.] Damien,

you let yourself be guided by the Holy Spirit,

like a son who obeys the will of the Father.

With your life and your missionary activities,

you express the kindness and mercy of Christ for
    each man,

awakening the beauty of the inner being,

which no disease, no deformity and no weakness can
    fully disfigure.

With your work and your preaching,

you recall that Jesus made his own the poverty and
    the suffering of men,

and that he revealed its mysterious value.

Intercede with Christ,

healer of the body and of the soul,

for our sick brothers and sisters,

in order that in their anguish and pain they will not
feel abandoned,

but instead, united to the Risen Lord and to His
Church,

discover that the Holy Spirit comes upon them,

and that in this way they may obtain the consolation
promised to the afflicted.

Amen.

(Prayer of Pope John Paul II at Beatification Mass for St. Damien of Molokai.)

Session 6

Transformed by His Cross

The Lord in His Scriptures

Nothing Can Separate Us from the Love of Christ

[W]e rejoice in our sufferings, knowing that suffering produces endurance, and endurance produces character, and character produces hope, and hope does not disappoint us, because God's love has been poured into our hearts through the Holy Spirit which has been given to us. **Romans 5:3-5.**

If God is for us, who is against us? He who did not spare his own Son but gave him up for us all, will he not also give us all things with him? Who shall separate us from the love of Christ? Shall tribulation, or distress, or persecution, or famine, or nakedness, or peril, or sword? No, in all these things we are more than conquerors through him who loved us. For I am sure that neither death, nor life, nor angels, nor principalities, nor things present, nor things to come, nor powers, nor height, nor depth, nor anything else in all creation, will be able to separate us from the love of God in Christ Jesus our Lord. **Romans 7:31-39.**

Put on . . . as God's chosen ones, holy and beloved, compassion, kindness, lowliness, meekness, and patience, forbearing one another and, if one has a complaint against another, forgiving each other . . . as the Lord has forgiven you . . . **Colossians 3:12-13.**

Soak in the Word.

Two Minutes of Silence.

Reflect . . .

The first two passages introducing this session
are from Paul's letter to the Romans, which he wrote
between 56 and 58 A.D., most likely from the city
of Corinth. This is Paul's longest letter and is ad-
dressed to an esteemed Christian community of
which he was not the founder, a community whose
bishop was St. Peter himself. Paul uses the letter
to introduce himself and to convey several themes
central to his preaching: sin, the law, faith, the grace
of salvation in Christ, and the relationship between
Israel and the Gentiles.

The few verses we have chosen for this session
are a tiny fragment from the letter to the Romans,
but they fit the purposes of this book and are rich in
significance.

St. Paul was well acquainted with suffering. In
the course of over thirty years of ministry he was
ridiculed, imprisoned, flogged, beaten with rods,
stoned and shipwrecked. Many times he went without adequate food, clothing or sleep. In the end he
died a martyr.

To Paul, none of this mattered—Christ was

everything. He knew that if he clung to his Lord, no suffering, no matter how great, could conquer him. He would gladly die with his Savior in order to share risen life with him.

Paul once wrote from prison: "I count everything as loss because of the surpassing worth of knowing Christ Jesus my Lord. For his sake I have suffered the loss of all things . . . in order that I may gain Christ and be found in him" (Philippians 3:8,9).

Paul was one of a whole host of martyrs in the early Church. We need to consider how easily we take for granted the practice of our faith, and to be mindful of the price others have paid for it, even in our own day (consider China, India and various Muslim nations).

The third passage introducing this session comes from the letter to the Colossians. It is a passage in which Paul appeals to the reader to show love and forgiveness. Suffering and forgiveness are intimately intertwined. It is not enough to accept suffering in our lives. We must also be able to extend forgiveness to those who cause us to suffer. Our model is Jesus in agony on the cross, who said with his dying breath, "Father, forgive them . . . ."

Pope Benedict XVI

There is no love without suffering—without the suffering of renouncing oneself, of the transformation and purification of self for true freedom. Where there is nothing worth suffering for, even life loses its value. The Eucharist—the center of our Christian being—is founded on Jesus' sacrifice for us; it is born from the suffering of love which culminated in the Cross. We live by this love that gives itself. It gives us the courage and strength to suffer with Christ and for him in this world, knowing that in this very way our life becomes great and mature and true.

(Year of St. Paul, Inaugural Homily, June 28, 2008.)

Catechism of the Catholic Church

2844 - Christian prayer extends to the *forgiveness of enemies,*[1] transfiguring the disciple by configuring him to his Master. Forgiveness is a high-point of Christian prayer; only hearts attuned to God's compassion can receive the gift of prayer. Forgiveness also bears witness that, in our world, love is stronger than sin. The martyrs of yesterday and today bear this witness to Jesus. Forgiveness is the fundamental condition of the reconciliation of the children of God with their Father and of men with one another.

---

[1] *Cf. Mt 5:43-44.*

The Lord in the Life of His People

Forgiveness Lights a Path of Hope

On September 22, 2008, I heard Immaculée Ilibagiza share her gripping story as a survivor of the Rwandan genocide of 1994. It is a story of suffering, love, faith, forgiveness and the incredible providence of a God who has counted every hair on our heads. All the quotes that follow, with the exception of the opening lines, are taken from that talk.

I heard the killers call my name.

They were on the other side of the wall, and less than an inch of plaster and wood separated us. Their voices were cold, hard, and determined.

"She's here ... we know she's here somewhere .... Find her—find Immaculée."

There were many voices, many killers. I could see them in my mind: my former friends and neighbors, who had always greeted me with love and kindness, moving through the house carrying spears and machetes and calling my name.

(Immaculée Ilibagiza in *Left to Tell,* Hay House, 2006, p. xix.)

There had long been tensions between Rwanda's two dominant tribes, the Hutus and the minority Tutsis, but when in 1994 the Hutu president died in a plane crash, the Tutsis were accused of shooting it down. A killing spree began in which up to a million Tutsis and their sympathizers were massacred. Hutu death squads went from house to house with machetes and spared no one, not even babies.

A parting gift

In that genocide, 22-year-old Immaculée Ilibagiza lost her father, her mother and two of her three brothers (one was out of the country). She survived because when her father got word of the first few attacks he told her to run and hide. "We are strong," he said to reassure her. "I am asking you to go."

"He handed me a red and white rosary," she said, "and I had a sense this was the last time I would see him."

Immaculée recalled her parents' goodness. "They cared about everybody," she said. "Discussions around our table were always about who needed help"—the woman in labor who needed to be driven to the hospital, the poor with whom they shared their clothes. "Actions of love," said Immaculée. "Otherwise, what do we live for?"

Faith in the midst of horror

Fleeing certain death, Immaculée and seven other women sought refuge in the home of a Hutu pastor who risked his life to hide them. Death squads threatened the pastor and searched his home several times. They pulled up carpets, broke through ceilings and plunged their machetes into suitcases in the chance that someone might be inside.

The women hid in a bathroom so tiny they had to take turns sitting and standing. They would pass a total of 91 days in this confinement. The pastor slid a wardrobe in front of the door to conceal it, but more than once the searchers came within inches of finding them. Immaculée began praying the rosary her father had given her "from morning to night." She also requested and received a Bible from the pastor. He marveled that the killers could search for hours and come so close, yet without finding the women. "I don't know what you are praying," he said, "but keep doing it."

The inner struggle

In addition to the violence going on in Immaculée's homeland, there was a war that raged in her own heart, a war between love and hatred. When she heard the voices of the killers outside, laughing and talking about killing "the Tutsi cockroaches," she fantasized "shooting them all" or "putting a bomb under the whole country and exploding it," she said.

124

She remembers feeling such anger that the muscles of her lips contorted. "I thought I would never know how to smile again."

When Immaculée would come to one of the countless passages in the Bible that speaks of love or forgiveness, she would stop and think, "but I don't love them" and flip to the next page. She prayed the Lord's Prayer "maybe two hundred times a day," but couldn't pray the words forgiving "those who trespass against us."

Immaculée recalled that at a pivotal moment in this inner war of the heart, she felt a voice say to her: "If you believe God is almighty, why don't you surrender, hand it over to Him?" Just then, "in my heart I knelt (I couldn't kneel physically) and prayed, 'If you know there is a way to forgive these people, help me.'"

Jesus' words on the cross then came to her: "Father, forgive them, for they know not what they do." She was able to see that the Hutu killers were practically possessed by a kind of evil madness. In later interviews, several of the perpetrators themselves commented on this. Said one, "When Satan is using you, you lose your mind. We were not ourselves."

As she contemplated these things, Immaculée felt her bitterness being lifted. Now she could love her enemy, she could pray for him.

125

"I forgive you."

In July of 1994, Immaculée and the other women at last escaped to the protection of French troops that had taken up a position not far from the pastor's house. The true test of the power of forgiveness would come months later, when Immaculée visited in prison the man who had orchestrated the murder of her family.

"He was dirty and swollen," she said. "I asked him to find a way to regret what he had done and to tell his children that he had done wrong." And then she looked him in the eye and said, "I forgive you."

Today, in all that she says and writes as she travels the world, Immaculée Ilibagiza proclaims the message that forgiveness, rooted in Christ, is mankind's one hope for healing and peace.

Following her talk, I spoke briefly with Immaculée Ilibagiza and told her about this faith-sharing series. I explained that one component of the program is to give loving service to others. I asked for a suggestion as to one simple thing people could do for their brothers and sisters in need.

Immaculée responded almost instantly: "Smile at them." This woman, who had once wondered if she would ever be able to smile again, was beaming.

Questions for Discussion

1. Reflecting on Paul's words and on your own experience and observations, discuss how suffering, painful as it is, can sometimes bring about positive fruit or growth in the lives of Christians. Can you think of a time when you saw this happen in your own life or the life of someone close to you? Discuss.

_____

_____

_____

_____

_____

_____

2. Service has been a component of this faith-sharing program because service is an integral part of what it means to be a disciple of Christ. Of course, it can take many forms, and that is worth thinking about.

- How might you give service if you were, like Immaculée Ilibagiza, confined to a tiny room for 91 days with seven other people?
- Shifting the focus a bit, how could you serve if you were confined to a wheelchair or a bed in a hospital or nursing home?

3. Now that this sixth and final session is drawing to a close, talk about some of the ways you and other group members have tried to carry out the component of service.

- What impact has this had on you?
- Have there been certain moments in service that have been particularly memorable?

_____

_____

_____

_____

_____

_____

_____

4. St. Paul obviously paid a high price in suffering
   for being a disciple of Christ.

   • When and how do we pay a price in our culture?
   • Where in the world can following Christ and his
     Church cost you your freedom or even your life?
   • Discuss what effect it might have on you and
     your faith to live in such a society.

5. Immaculée Ilibagiza manages to forgive the man who arranged for the death of her family. But hers is not a cheap, "blank check," "everything's okay" form of forgiveness. How does her approach to forgiveness avoid simply letting the perpetrator off the hook, and what does that tell us about authentic forgiveness?

_____

_____

_____

_____

_____

_____

Group Prayers of Intercession

8 to 10 minutes

Closing Prayer

For Those Who Suffer for the Name of Christ

Jesus, you continue to gather together and sanctify
　　suffering of all kinds:
that of the sick, of those who die in hardship,
　　of all who experience discrimination;
but the sufferings which shine out above all others
　　are those endured for your name.

By the sufferings of martyrs, bless your Church;
may their blood become the seed of new Christians.

We firmly believe that their sufferings,

even if they appear to be total defeat,

will bring true victory to your Church.

Lord, grant constancy to our persecuted brethren!

(From the Meditations for the Way of the Cross composed by Cardinal Joseph Zen, Bishop of Hong Kong, celebrated by Pope Benedict XVI on Good Friday of 2008.)

Appendix

Suggestions for Service

As stated in the Introduction, we are not truly disciples of Christ until we take seriously his words: "Truly, I say to you, as you did it to one of the least of these my brethren, you did it to me" (Matthew 25:40).

With a smile and an open heart, we are called to be the hands and feet of Christ in the world, especially to those in need. But sometimes we need a little help getting started. Here are a few suggestions:

Ask your pastor about needs in the parish community

"Charity begins at home," and in the life of the Church that's your parish. Your pastor can help you learn who are the lonely, the elderly, the sick or homebound in your community. He can tell you who needs Holy Communion, the human kindness of a visit, and who has material needs. You might also ask if there are parishioners who need a ride to Mass because of age, health, or special needs.

Contact Catholic Charities

Consider offering some volunteer time

to Catholic Charities, which has agencies throughout the country. To find one near you, visit **www.catholiccharitiesusa. org,** click on "Who We Are" and then "Local Agency Directory."

Check your Yellow Pages listings under "Social Service Organizations" or "Volunteer Services"

You may be surprised to learn how many opportunities for service exist in your community: Meals on Wheels, Habitat for Humanity, Birthright or other crisis pregnancy centers, food pantries, homeless shelters, Catholic Worker houses, and more.

Pay attention to what is "right under your nose"

Sometimes we can get tied up in a knot trying to decide where to go and what to do, when there's an elderly neighbor next door or a nursing home a few blocks away. No doubt, there are people close by that are lonely and would love a visit.

May the ancient witness be renewed:

"See how they love one another!"

The Discipleship Series

Novo Millennio Press